HELLO DARKNESS, IT'S ME.

JUSTIN TRINITY

333:MIDNIGHT BOOKS

CONTENTS

from magical me to magical you.

to my Warriors and Dragons of the Moon.

Hi! From the bottom of my heart, I want to thank you for being here with me in this moment.

I want to thank you for being brave enough to look inwards, and for processing the differences between who you are, and who you were conditioned to believe you are.

This collection was written while going through some of the most difficult times of my life, but through these words, I discovered strength I never knew I was capable of having.

I hope that by reading these pieces, you will be inspired to see your own life experiences in a new light and move towards achieving your own version of greatness.

I want you to know you are loved and appreciated. Thank you for existing and growing with me.

You Used To Be A Dreamer.

What happened to you?

You used to be a dreamer.

Now, it's the same damn thing every day.

Wake up. Barely get by. Come home. Cry yourself to sleep. Then, rinse and repeat.

Oh, I get it. You're tired. You're exhausted. You don't see an end to the misery, and you just want it to stop.

So, let's make it stop-

and no, we're not taking the easy way out.

We're heading straight into The Abyss.

Straight towards everything you fear, because you know what?

I still believe in you. I always have, but at this point, I can't help but wonder, if not now, then when?

And if not you, then who? Because no one's here to save you.

No one.

You can't be upset with the world for not being here when you aren't even here for yourself.

So, I'll ask again, IF NOT NOW, THEN WHEN?

The Abyss.

Once again, I find myself floating in an empty space,

A space between who I was and who I could become.

Where the horizon ahead of me is alluded by a sunset of uncertainty,

where gravity keeps me suspended without forward momentum,

and where I question if I'll be able to move forward into the unknown,

or if I'll be damned as a bystander to who I could have been.

Standing over the edge where ambitions decay,

and mediocrity infectiously envelops-

where the only guarantee is a poisonous kiss of death.

At some point, we all end up peering over this breathtaking view of the unknown,

and at some point,

we'll all have to ask ourselves-

"Am I going to jump?"

"What's the cost of me not jumping?"

"Could I live with myself if I don't?"

"Or will I suffer a slow, quiet, and painful death ignoring what makes me feel alive?"

Whether we jump or not,

we're still making a choice and are sacrificing something.

What sacrifices will you be able to live with?

What if I told you this story isn't finished yet?

What if I told you those beautiful dreams aren't bullshit and ARE possible.

Would you believe me?

Me neither,

but at this point,

what choice do we have left?

To accept defeat?

HELL NO.

We're not settling.

As long as your heart is beating,

this is far from over.

There's a fiery volcano hidden deep within your depths,

waiting to be awakened.

You're so powerfully beautiful.

You're so amazingly full of life.

This rollercoaster of a story is just getting to the best parts.

It's far from over.

Who are you when the world is quiet?

When the roads have cleared, and the Moon has neared-

Who is the person that gazes toward the wishful sky?

Wonder as you might,

what do you wish for tomorrow to bring?

What are you willing to do in order to make that happen?

Because I promise you,

a wish without effort is nothing but a wish.

Your life doesn't magically change for the better overnight.

Your change won't come from waiting for an opportunity or miracle.

Always remember;

You ARE the opportunity. You ARE the miracle.

Your life will change a tiny bit every day when your actions reflect the future you want to create.

Do you want a lover that's loyal, responsible, and passionate?

Then, be loyal, responsible, and passionate about yourself.

Do you want to make fun, growth-focused friends who are full of life?

Then, be fun, growth-focused, and full of life yourself.

Do you want to have breathtaking days ahead of you that you'll be so proud to experience?

Then, make the sacrifices today to have those beautiful tomorrows.

Do you want to have a life that makes you cry tears of joy?

Then, look around you and be grateful that you have this moment and a heart that will push you towards that life.

Become the change you wish to see.

Be patient, be gentle, be open-minded,

and let go of what used to be.

You try your best to blend in, but you are planets away from the ordinary.

You try to run from it.

You try to ignore that there's something within you that burns for excitement,

but you do whatever you can to extinguish those flames.

You know that if you accept your calling from within that it'll require you to do something about it,

and that terrifies you-

but I assure you that nothing is more terrifying than doing absolutely nothing and spending your life struggling to convince yourself that it's okay.

NOW is the time to make a move.

NOW is the time to make a change.

NOW is your time.

You're special.

You have experiences and perspectives that are entirely unique to you.

It's okay to break away from everything you've known.

It's okay to be who you were always called to be.

Hey, you're settling again.

Look, it's okay.

I get it.

Waiting sucks.

Hearing, "It'll be here. Just be patient,"

over and over again,

sucks.

Sitting within the uncomfortable feelings of not knowing when, how, what, and why DEFINITELY sucks-

but if you were looking to hear anything different,

I'm sorry to disappoint,

but it'll be here. Just be patient. (lol)

The longer you entertain what's not for you,

the longer you'll have to wait for what is.

The longer you take to match the energy of what you deserve,

the longer it'll take to attract that same energy toward you.

You can't receive what you aren't even mirroring yourself.

Now reread those last three sentences again.

Fly away, little Dragon.

Life is so much more than the view from your nest.

I know familiarity gave you safety,

but it's time to give it a rest.

Fly away, little Dragon.

The best has yet to come,

from the mountains to the valleys, to the shadows of the Sun.

Fly away, little Dragon.

I know it's frightening from this height,

but there's nothing scarier than living a life where you never took flight.

Choose differently, or the cycle repeats.

Choose differently, or the cycle repeats.

Choose differently, or the cycle repeats.

CHOOSE DIFFERENTLY.

Do you see the patterns?

Do you see why people fail time after time?

Do you see how powerful it is to become mindful of your thoughts?

Do you see how powerful it is to become mindful of the emotions that come from your thoughts?

Do you see how powerful it is to realize your actions are powered by your emotions?

All patterns and cycles are led by inner programming that can be reprogrammed by you.

A thought only holds merit when you give it power by feeding into it.

We all have intrusive and paranoid thoughts,

but how we handle them makes all the difference.

You'll never finish the puzzle if you don't put it together one piece at a time.

Meaning,

stop trying to have it all figured out before you even begin.

You're never going to be ready.

You're never going to have most of the answers.

You're never going to feel qualified,

but you already are!

Who you are in this very moment is all the credibility you'll ever need.

Screw anyone that says otherwise.

The clarity and pieces will come together as you slowly progress forward.

Stop waiting for an epiphany that may never happen.

This IS your epiphany!

GO!

Do you see how much your perspective differs from everyone else in your environment?

Do you feel your body rejecting this way of living that isn't serving you anymore?

It's the same things happening repeatedly,

but they play out in different scenarios.

Do you see it?

I can tell you want more.

You want fulfillment. You want to break away from the cycles of pretending.

You want to go after a feeling most don't think exists, but deep down, you know does.

You want to follow a trail that's invisible to most.

A path that makes you look crazy,

but I'm here to tell you that maybe you're not so crazy after all.

Maybe,

you're perfectly sane and putting down your mask is the most sane thing you could ever do.

Maybe,

the craziest thing you could ever do is to keep pretending that a "normal" life is perfectly fine with you,

when that's the furthest thing from the truth.

Stardust settled where I used to fondly gaze upon my future.

"I wish... I wish..." I'd whisper,

but as time flowed, no wish was ever granted.

The only thing that came to fruition was wasted time.

Lots. Of wasted. Time.

As I gazed upon a future in which I never acted upon my desires-

I saw the regrets and disappointments I'd carry.

The anger, the resentment, the ways I didn't smile like I once did,

and the way my eyes reflected the disconnect between my future and my "could have been" future.

But as I open my eyes,

stardust begins to settle where I presently have a choice-

a choice for a future where I run towards every desire I felt was meant for me,

a choice to accept that wishing upon a star without manifesting through effort is a wish that's sadly wasted.

A choice to become the granter of my own wishes.

When it's time to make the judgment call,

which path will you choose?

To go down the path of what you've already known and greatly risk repeating the cycle,

or will you take the leap into the unknown and sacrifice your comfort?

What if the "right time" never comes?

What if the moment you've been waiting for never happens?

Is that worth the risk?

Don't you realize that not deciding is also a decision?

Take your power back and learn to trust that you'll always be okay no matter what you decide.

That no matter what,

you'll always be safe,

ESPECIALLY if you choose the scariest option,

because that will, in turn,

bring you closer to the life you dream of than if you decided to play it safe.

Take the leap.

Your highest self believes in you.

Where are you going?!

The path meant for you is that way.

It's never been, Free Will vs. Destiny.

It's always been your Free Will to CHOOSE your Destiny.

Your Destiny calls to you in hopes that you choose to follow it,

but how many times will you ignore your path until it stops calling out to you?

If you're confused about finding your path, the solution is much simpler than you think.

All it takes is for you to finally start gaining trust within yourself.

And how do you do that, you ask?

You do that by learning the power of saying no to what doesn't *feel right* and yes to what does.

The more you do that,

the more trust you gain within yourself,

strengthening your ability to sense and follow your path.

Trust yourself.

Your Destiny awaits you.

One of the best parts about being a 'nobody'-

is that you can be whoever you want to be at any time.

Ask yourself,

how does this person dress?

What types of people will they allow into their life?

What types of love do they accept and walk away from?

What beautiful places do they want to travel to?

What beliefs will they fight for?

What do their daily habits look like?

What habits did they have to sacrifice to make room for their new life?

It's a fun idea worth playing with because one of the best parts about being a 'nobody'-

is that once you decide who you're going to be,

no one can ever tell you differently.

Sometimes,

living up to your potential may require you to accept that you will make many unhappy.

It may require you to accept that everyone won't be able to come with you,

not because they're not good enough,

but because your paths aren't heading in the same direction.

It may require you to accept that you will feel pain no matter what.

You're either going to feel pain from shedding the life you once lived,

or you will feel pain from losing the life you once dreamed of.

Which path of pain will you choose?

What defines you aren't the moments that left behind shattered glass and a broken home.

What defines you is how you choose to move forward when all you have left are the pieces of what used to be.

With all your pain, tears, and fears, who will you be today?

Will you make decisions based on a void of sadness, guilt, and regrets?

Will you dismiss yourself, strangers, and the people that care for you?

Will you take it out on them? Or will you show compassion and embrace them instead of running away?

How will you redefine love? How will you redefine what it means to be who you are?

Whatever you choose, always remember this;

You deserve the love and compassion you so desperately needed from your past, but the past doesn't define you, and it never did.

It only seemed that way because it's what you subconsciously chose to believe, but that isn't the case.

You're not going to let that happen anymore, are you?

No. No, you're not.

This time, even though it'll be difficult, things will be different.

They'll be different because that's the only choice we're giving ourselves now.

It'll all be worth it. I promise.

Listen to me...

this is the moment that'll decide the rest of our lives.

We're in the middle of a bridge that's cracking beneath our feet and now it's time to finally decide.

You can go back to the comforts of predictability, safety, and your sense of certainty-

or you can take my hand and run with me towards a place where the only certainty is uncertainty.

I mean, we already know how one side turns out, right?

I don't know about you, but that side to me feels like purgatory-

and as for the unknown...

What if those imaginative crazy ideas could come true?

Isn't that alone worth the leap of faith?

Just know, no matter what you choose, I'll support it if you're genuinely content with your decision, okay?

The bridge is beginning to collapse.

Which direction will you finally choose?

As I lay on the floor and look up to the ceiling,

I can't help but wonder if this will all pay off.

A part of me has faith that it will, but another part of me, which was born from several unfortunate events, can't help but have a cynical stance.

Tomorrow isn't promised, and neither are stressless, peaceful, and financially stable days, but what if I was able to believe in the unbelievable?

What if it was never "seeing is believing," but instead, "believing is seeing?"

Perhaps, I must be somewhat out of my mind to believe that one day the life I once knew will completely turn around,

but regardless, I still carry on toward the unknown.

"Nothing is impossible," and that fable of a belief alone is enough for me to carry on through The Abyss.

If I give up now, I'll never know.

So, here's to not giving up.

Here's to believing in the unbelievable.

I see you,

Darkness.

I see you, Darkness.

And, like me, you're so beautifully terrifying.

Like me, you awoke one night to find yourself searching for guidance within a starless sky.

Like me, there was plenty of sleep to be had, but it was never enough to nourish your starvation of rest.

And like me, you felt coldly rejected by the Sun's warmth while the mystical aura of the Moon embraced you with open arms.

The lack of healthy love we experienced created a void we attempted to fill from within a world we so desperately wanted to love us.

We yearned to be loved so badly that self-love wasn't even an afterthought.

Sadly, we never knew we could be our own friends, parents, and lovers.

We never knew we could heal by allowing our pain to flow through us instead of pretending it wasn't there.

And we never knew our darkest shadows could give us the strength to confront our most paralyzing fears.

I see you, Darkness.

And, like me, you realize that a painful life doesn't have to be a life sentence.

You realize that you are not alone, and you never were.

We were born from within the fires of a home that managed to look
so pristine on the outside,

but was burned to a crisp within.

A home where the only embrace of warmth came after a fiery combustion of emotional and verbal hostility.

A home where each gasp of breath taken within the smog of tension
slowly suffocated our pure innocence and hopeful imaginations.

As children, we had no choice but to weather the ashes of chaos
around us.

We stayed quiet as we held on while waiting for the frequent storms
to pass.

We held on to our hearts that cried for unwavering affection.

We held on to our tiny little fantasies of a day we'd be loved for
simply existing as who we are.

We held on to the possibility that it might not always be like this.

We held on within the fires that burned us to our cores,

but revealed we have such a beautiful heart of gold.

Truth be told,

I'm terrified.

I'm terrified of dying before I get to express the many things that are erupting from my soul.

I'm terrified of feeling guilty for overcoming my fears and traumas,

while those I care for are still stuck within the same cycles.

I'm terrified of unintentionally hurting those I had to distance my-self from for me to heal.

I'm terrified of opening my heart,

because I worry that I'm too dull and uninteresting.

I'm terrified of only being a temporary experience instead of being held as someone's eternity.

Truth be told,

I'm terrified.

But I'm going to continue moving forward anyways.

I fell deep into your silence.

A place where laughter hides and smiles have fallen ill.

A place where the Moon is always new, and the Sun is never full.

A place once full of life and beautiful horizons,

but is now as desolate as Pluto.

A place I could hold you,

but feel the vast emptiness of being worlds away.

Is this what it's like to love someone who will never truly love you?

The darkest nights create the brightest stars,

but out of all I've lost,

I never lost my heart.

I look out from the shadows and wonder, "Why?"

"Why does it take misery and pain for me to see the light?"

"Is this part of the plan?"

"Was this always meant to be?"

"Am I supposed to break to find the best parts of me?"

"If who I was isn't who I'm to become-

Does that mean that I could be as bright as the Sun?"

You may have everyone else fooled, but not me.

I see you as clearly as the teardrops that silently drop from your precious face.

I see the beautiful, authentic, and masterpiece of a mess you are.

I see how much you struggle to hold it together when every part of you needs to fall apart.

I see you, and damn, are you beautiful.

Right here. Right now. You don't have to pretend.

Right here. Right now. You're safe to fall completely apart.

And you want to know why?

It's because you'll come back together in ways you never imagined.

It's because sometimes,

falling completely apart is how we can finally become whole.

I wish I could hate you.

I wish I could make you the target of my broken heart, but that wouldn't be me.

The anger I tried so hard to embrace was only to cover up the fact that I'm deeply saddened for letting go of someone I was deeply in love with.

I could never hold negative feelings toward you.

I could never lie to myself or lie to you-

because in the end, I'd mostly be hurting myself.

Truthfully, what we had was beautiful, and what makes it more heartbreaking is that we both know we could have chosen to move forward together, but that's not the case.

I have faith that one day we'll figure it out,

but maybe, in another lifetime.

Your fingers slip one by one as you grasp onto toxic relationships that hurt you repeatedly.

You're afraid to be without them,

and that's perfectly okay.

I understand...

I understand how conflicting and confusing it is for you.

I understand how your desperate need to love and be loved can't help but be unleashed,

but unfortunately, that need is being used against you.

And even worse, they know it,

but they simply don't care enough to set you free.

Does that sound like love to you? Does that sound like something you deserve?

Hmm, I don't think so.

So, trust me when I say it's okay to finally let go.

Of course, it's going to be scary.

Of course, it's going to hurt,

but I promise you that it'll lead you to connections so beautiful that you'll wish you had let go sooner.

So, please, let go.

You know...

I don't recall the last time you simply just took care of yourself.

When was the last time you fed your soul the love it so deservingly needs?

When was the last time you didn't let guilt convince you that you don't deserve nice things?

Because it's the complete opposite of the truth.

When was the last time you told yourself "I LOVE YOU,"

and truly meant it?

If not yesterday...

If not today...

then when?

I don't like seeing you like this,

and I know you don't either.

It makes me sad because you're so beautiful and deserve nothing but peace and unconditional love.

You deserve to feel whole.

You deserve nice things.

You deserve loving experiences.

They're trying not to think about it,

which slowly leads to drinking 'bout it.

Their ego tries to run around it,

but Regret and Shame are massive mountains.

They couldn't face themselves or you,

so, they chose to wear a mask instead.

They distorted what was real and true,

so, your heart ached and second-guessed.

These complicated situations cut deep within your head.

Please accept and let them go so they won't bleed on what's ahead-

I know it's hard to think about it,

but it's best for you to feel throughout it.

I promise, there's no way around it,

because Mistrust and Pain are massive mountains.

You know that deep, intense, unconditional love you so easily hand to others?

What if you gave that to yourself as well?

What if you looked at your scars and kissed them?

What if you promised yourself, "I'll never leave your side," and you kept it?

What if you looked at your reflection and said, "I completely adore you regardless of how you look."

What if you were all you ever needed, and everything else was the cherry on top?

What if you realized the love you so desperately desired was within you all along?

What if the key to inner peace was knowing you'll be taken care of by yourself and the universe, no matter what's happening around you?

What if you chose happiness in this present moment instead of chasing it?

Wouldn't that be beautiful?

Wouldn't that give you joy?

Somewhere in time,

I promised myself I'd be someone I'd look up to,

but then I had company with a mixture of misery,

which only loved me when I'm fragile.

So, for this love,

all my healing has to stop?

For this love,

it gets worse when I'm better?

For this love,

all that matters is "together"?

But is it still love if my heart drops?

Is it still love if I embrace the sunny weather?

Is it still love if Darkness isn't forever?

My shadow was my only friend.

Tearful nights, we'd play pretend-

Pretending we were someone loved without conditions or an end.

My shadow was my only friend.

A child who was questioning-

something's severely wrong with me 'cause nothing else is making sense.

And why wouldn't you hug me?

Your glares made me feel ugly.

No hesitations,

physical altercations.

You'd feel bad,

then tell me you loved me.

Safety was inconsistent,

love turned codependent-

I learned to love from a distance since "love" could leave within an instant.

How many more?

How many more nights will your tears go to waste on people that happily took everything,

but spitefully gave nothing in return?

How many more times will you betray your heart by entrusting it to those that never intended to fortify it,

but instead, manipulate its kindness?

How many more times will you feed life into dead, empty promises from those without integrity or the character to back them up?

I say all of this with so much love in my heart.

Please wake up, love.

Those people do not love you.

Love is supposed to encourage your health and growth,

not starve you and trap you within a lack mentality.

No matter how bad it gets.

No matter how dark it becomes...

You must hold on to the make-believe fairytale that things DO eventually get better.

You must hold on to the belief that your value in this life is absolutely priceless.

You must hold on to the belief that there are people out there that won't be able to live as vibrantly without your beautiful presence after meeting you.

To the belief that even though it's nice to have outside reassurance-

that your worth is most importantly dependent on you.

You must hold on to love and how it can be used to be a safe space for all your darkest moments.

No matter how ugly this world can be,

you must hold on to the belief that the beauty found within the darkest corners will always outshine.

This world needs you,

so do I,

and so do you.

Why do you keep allowing people to walk all over you?

Why do you keep settling for the same ugly behaviors and treatment?

While you think about that, I'll tell you why they keep doing what they're doing.

It's because they believe they'll always be able to get away with it.

It's because they believe you don't love yourself enough for them to treat you like a decent human.

Think about that...

Your vulnerabilities and desires to love unconditionally are being used to make them feel better about being a shitty person.

I don't know about you, but that doesn't sound like love to me.

That sounds cruel.

So. Very. Cruel.

So, please, choose yourself for once.

That isn't love, and you know it.

You deserve so much better.

Now act like it.

Teardrops fall from her ruby-colored cheeks like the prettiest rose you've ever seen,

but her misty eyes tell the story of a silent violence.

She doesn't need watering.

She doesn't need sunlight.

She needs quiet,

and she needs a friend,

but her thoughts constantly swarm like a savage hurricane-

ripping apart every sense of stability she's ever known.

Calmness escapes her grasp as she does her best to plant her roots beneath the unsettled dirt,

but her fragile frame is weakening as she cries for a supportive embrace she believes doesn't exist.

She looks to the hilltops,

but only finds what she already expected in the first place...

No one.

She knows every storm eventually comes to an end,

but what happens when no one knows the storm even transpired?

What happens to the lonely, beautiful flower, then?

What if the endless Forest of Darkness and misery wasn't endless?

What if you didn't need to know exactly where you are heading,

but simply just need to walk in a direction?

What if that "direction" consisted of making small, daily changes?

What if the key to a life of peace is your ability to keep moving forward no matter what?

What if you decided today that the beliefs you've carried all this way due to horrible experiences weren't beliefs you had to believe anymore?

What if you chose a new identity and never looked back?

What if you chose a new set of beliefs to represent what it means to be *you*?

You did me so wrong.

And I didn't ever say a thing,

and didn't throw dirt on your name,

but you still villainized me.

I can feel your guilt and shame,

why are you so fixated on this grave?

Is this the hill you choose to die on?

How could you villainize me?

I loved you even through your most profound flaws.

I was sure of you even in your moments of uncertainty.

How could you turn on me so quickly?

Why would you villainize me?

Why is it that you give people chance after chance,

but when it comes to you,

you're left to heal on your own?

That doesn't seem fair.

It doesn't seem fair that you lighten and embrace the mistakes of others,

but when it comes to you-

it's almost like you're not allowed to be human.

Why is that?

Don't you deserve the same energy and patience you give to others?

Isn't it time you start choosing those that happily and consistently choose you?

Isn't it time you start choosing yourself?

If I'm being honest,

to tell the truth, I'm really scared.

I gaze into the mirror and question if I'm even there.

It's such a dangerous game to try to prove that you're alive,

but what I fear the most is feeling dead living a lie.

I've been drowning in my thoughts-

Guess I've forgotten how to swim.

Guess I've forgotten how to breathe.

Guess I've forgotten that my shadows were only supposed to be half of me.

And if I'm being honest,

I'm not sure what tomorrow holds.

Is this what it's like to live a life that's cold and froze?

Do I dive into the deep?

Do I dive into the unknown?

Do I dive within myself-

so I don't feel I'm as alone?

You may have been convinced that you were small,

insignificant,

and nothing but a bluff,

but consider this...

Why do you think people have been so adamant on making sure you believe you're no one special?

Why do you think they're so loud about your failures,

but grow silent when you have any success?

I'll tell you why.

It's because your existence triggers them.

It's because your existence is a threat to their own insecurities.

Your existence is a mirror to their own failures,

fears,

and unwillingness to change.

And you want to know what some people do when triggered by a mirror that forces them to acknowledge their insecurities?

They do whatever they can to break and get rid of it.

You've been having to go through hell to find yourself.

You've been suffering more than most to find who you truly are.

What you've experienced and are currently experiencing hasn't all been for nothing, though.

The things you've seen,

the emotions you've deeply felt,

and the places you've been,

are meant to turn into something that adds gentleness and care for yourself and the world around you.

Those hurtful nights you've spent tearfully looking up towards the Moon?

You'll use those as a reminder to accept nothing less than your worth and to treat people how they deserve.

Those times you've expressed yourself only to be misunderstood?

You'll use that to make sure others feel genuinely seen and heard.

And those chapters of darkness you lived?

You'll turn into a light that brightens up the rest of your days.

I assure you,

it has not been for nothing.

Every day I wake with the hope that the hours will fly by.

That night will fall, and the outer worldly demons will go into hiding-

so I can slip back into a heavy slumber where I'm safe from my thoughts.

I'd rather dream my life away than be forced to face reality,

but deep down, I know that wouldn't be fair to this world,

and it wouldn't be fair to me either.

I can't run away anymore.

I must face this darkness and awaken my inner light.

I must learn to accept that I am exactly what this world needs,

and that I've always been more than good enough.

Always.

- written by me & my amazing, beautiful friend, Aisha Glory.

I've always wondered how things would have turned out if I had a consistent and healthy parent in my life.

I've always wondered what it would be like to feel unwavering, unconditional love.

To never have to question whether you were a burden to your own parents.

To feel like a gift that was meant to be here,

instead of a burden.

What would it be like to not have your heart broken so much to the point that your heart bleeds into each relationship you try to foster?

What would it be like to not feel like a stranger to someone you thought you were supposed to be close to?

Most days it's easier to push it to the back of my mind,

but some days,

it hurts to think about the painful void it has left in its wake.

This is one of those "some days."

What keeps me up at night aren't the shadows,

the traumas,

or the past experiences I've overcome.

What keeps me up at night are the children crying themselves to sleep and are mentally, emotionally, and physically abused in a place they're supposed to feel safe.

What keeps me up at night are the beautiful and loving human beings that sleep on the streets,

and feel that they aren't worthy of being considered a human.

What keeps me up at night are the broken hearts that show up day after day with a half-smile on their face,

even though their spirit wants to collapse.

As we all grow together,

I urge you to take the time to truly see those of us who may be too afraid, tired, or weak to speak up.

I urge you to let them know that their existence is valid and that their experiences don't define them.

I urge you to show them that good people and love in this world are never lost,

even in the darkest of times.

Don't you dare give up on us.

The entire world may not deserve to experience your precious heart,

but there are plenty of us here that do.

There are plenty of us you haven't met yet that would be in awe that someone like you even exists.

Plenty of us want nothing more than to see you shine as the vibrant star you are.

You say you can't see a path in front of you?

Well then listen to the sound of my voice...

KEEP MOVING FORWARD!

You're not done yet.

The world needs you.

YOU need you!

Everything before this was just the prequel.

The main story is finally beginning.

Little by little.

Day by day.

From now until forever,

you're on your way.

I'd rather die before I ever settle.

The way I see it, you're already partially dead to some extent if you sell yourself short.

So, I must do this.

I must keep going.

Time isn't up,

and I have yet to see what I'm truly made of.

I'm not doing this because I'm afraid to die.

I'm doing this to discover if I was ever even alive, to begin with.

I'm doing this because, at one point,

I looked up to the stars,

and I made a wish,

I wished for the strength to become something greater than myself.

I wished for the courage to desire and actively pursue my desires.

I wished upon a star that one day I'll become a star.

I wished to burn brightly through the night skies.

I wished to be alive.

Little did we know,

we'd eventually become the very Darkness we used to be so terrified of as a child.

Little did we know,

the monster that was hiding beneath our bed was real,

but the monster wasn't quite what we imagined-

the monster was inside of us the entire time.

It was our own minds.

It would lie to us, play tricks on us, and make us see and believe things that weren't even there.

It would make us run away from the things that gave us life because we were so afraid that we'd die if we ever lost them.

It would convince us of a reality that was completely fabricated in shadows and misfortune-

but little did we know,

we also had the power to train our minds to create a reality of love,

life, and beautiful experiences.

Look around you.

You've outgrown this place.

It's not inherently wrong;

it's just limiting who you are.

It's limiting your soul.

It's limiting who you could potentially become.

It's limiting you from realizing that the world isn't as scary as it seems,

and you're so much fucking bigger than you've been leading everyone to believe,

especially yourself.

So, wake up.

WAKE. UP.

You owe it to yourself.

You owe it to your one life.

You owe it to those who've been hoping to find someone like you one day.

Wake up.

You're ready,

and you always were.

I'm incredibly proud of you for the person you were,

who you are,

and who you're becoming.

You didn't come this far just to come this far.

You're a Warrior and Dragon of the Moon.

Darkness always returns,

but you chose to learn from the Darkness to strengthen your relationship with the light.

As a Warrior and Dragon of the Moon,

it's your responsibility to elevate yourself so you can pay it forward and strengthen others.

So, thank you for being here.

Thank you for fighting.

Thank you for being living proof that miracles DO happen.

Hello Darkness,

it's me.

Hello Darkness, it's me.

I'm finally here, and I'm here to stay.

It's funny how things change.

I felt so small. So powerless. So hopeless.

I felt like I was unlovable, like all the horrible things I experienced were because they were what I deserved, and like the world didn't care for me to be alive.

But all those feelings were wrong.

It took time to realize that someone's mistreatment of me didn't reflect my value but instead reflected the way they valued themselves.

It took time to realize I was infinitely more sophisticated and memorable than I initially believed.

It took time to realize my most painful experiences were some of my most significant awakenings to who I was all along.

Thank you, Darkness,

for showing me it's okay to feel again.

Thank you for showing me which corners of my mind would lead to inner freedom.

Thank you for always being here even when I believed I would be forever alone.

Thank you, Darkness.

I'm finally here, and was always meant to be.

It's funny until it isn't.

They point, they laugh, then whisper about your moments of authenticity and vulnerability.

It's as if they know you better than you know yourself.

It's as if they assume that people can't change and would rather choose comfort over uncertainty, just like they did.

It's as if they had you all figured out...

the loner who had their own interests and developed their own opinions.

What a loser, right?

Well, they're wrong. Dead wrong.

Little do they know,

people like you change the world.

People like you see outside the lines of "what you're supposed to do."

People like you realize the power of observation and self-reinvention.

Little do they know,

people like you become the leaders of the future.

One day you're going to look back at these moments,

and you're going to be incredibly proud for stepping into the unknown.

You'll remember all the moments of uncertainty where you laid silently in your room, wondering if it would all pay off.

You'll remember the countless tears that streamed down your face as you carefully climbed back up from your moments of exhaustion.

You'll realize that who you are is mythical.

The obstacles you overcame were things most people couldn't fathom clearing nearly as gracefully.

You're someone deserving of being celebrated,

just for the sheer fact that your fiery spirit is proof that magic does exist.

One day you're going to look back and be so thankful that you became your own wish come true.

This may seem weird but do me a favor and genuinely speak to your reflection, and say:

"I'm sorry I was so hard on you."

"I'm sorry I wasn't there for you in the ways you needed me to be."

"I'm sorry I talked you into accepting the bare minimum from others."

"I forgive you for putting your needs to the side for people that ultimately only cared for themselves."

"I promise that from now on, I'll wholeheartedly be devoted to you and your needs."

"I love you, unconditionally."

"I deserve unconditional love, and it's as simple as that."

I don't just want to fall in love,

I want to trust in love.

I want to be safe in love.

I want to build a home in love.

A home where you don't have to hide.

A home where the truth brings you closer.

A home where you have the space to be yourself,

but also, the transparency to remove your walls.

I don't just want to fall in love,

I want to stand in it while by your side.

You were meant to evolve while in the fire,

not while standing around it.

Embrace the pain.

Face the fears.

Step into the unknown of who you'll be once you step out.

You owe it to yourself to say,

"ENOUGH IS ENOUGH."

You owe it to yourself to look around you and realize that your circumstances are unacceptable.

You owe it to yourself to step into the fire and burn away all the fears and limiting beliefs that kept you "safe" in chaos.

You owe it to yourself.

Step into the fire.

Shhh, do you hear that?

Do you hear the faint whispers that call to you from within the depths of your soul?

Do you hear them whispering that it's finally okay to let go of your heavy burdens?

That it's finally okay to step towards the unknown and let go of your shattered past?

Do you hear them whispering how loved you are and how fucking precious every cell of your existence is?

Do you hear them softly say how they want to squeeze you so tight that the tears you've locked away burst from within your overfilled heart?

Shhh, are you listening?

Goodbye, memories.

You weren't all bad,

but even so,

what's the point of carrying you with me today?

I need to begin living *in the now.*

I need to open my eyes to the world right before me.

Just because certain things have happened doesn't mean you get to
have a say in my life.

I've realized that I was holding onto things that are more afraid of
being forgotten than I was of forgetting them-

but that has now come to an end.

I choose a new beginning.

I choose me.

I choose to leave the comforts of what I've known.

I choose to find joy in not knowing what's to come.

She's not the woman you used to know.

She's not her adorable laugh or her pretty little smile.

She's not her blissful tears or her shadowy insecurities.

She's not her moments of weakness or her memories of sadness.

No, she's evolved so far past those.

She's evolved deeply beneath the surface.

She's the eternal fire that refuses to die.

She's the Mother of Life and the Angel of Death.

She's everything you were too afraid to honestly acknowledge.

A woman like her would never feel safe sharing her power with someone who innately feels threatened by it.

This world needs more people like you.

It needs more people that take pride in valuing themselves and others.

It needs more people that view sharing love as a win-win situation.

It needs more people that fill their own cups and let them lovingly overflow into the cups of others.

It needs more people that not only give a shit about how others feel but also do their best to prove that others care about how they feel.

It needs more honest,

pure,

and genuine expression.

It needs you.

It always needed you.

It always will.

Embrace that you're the change this world needs.

At the end of the day, the only person who can free you from your traumas and fears is you.

Not your family, not your friends, and not even your lover.

Just you.

It takes reminding yourself every single day that you ARE loved.

You ARE worthy.

You ARE someone that deserves nice things and experiences.

At the end of the day,

you're going to have to not only carry that weight but also embrace it in a way that makes you more substantial than you were way before.

At the end of the day,

the way you choose to face your Darkness is what will decide your future to come.

You were made for this.

You were born for this.

You were always destined to become more significant than your circumstances.

Saying 'no' to you was me finally saying 'yes' to myself.

It was me finally stepping away from your shadow and realizing that I shined so much brighter on my own.

I realized that you wanted me smaller because you were afraid to face the reality of how you truly felt about yourself,

which was that you felt powerless and unsure of who you were-

So, you took it out on me and tried to make me feel unsure of myself to gain some delusional sense of power.

I realized that you didn't want what was best for me.

You only wanted what was best for you under the disguise of what was best for me.

Now, I choose me.

I choose to evolve through empowerment.

I choose to accept myself and others for who they truthfully are.

I choose love over fear.

Saying 'no' to you was one of the most important 'yeses' I ever said.

This is YOUR era.

This is your era of embracing the power of saying "no."

This is your era of knowing when it's time to take a stand or walk away.

This is your era of loving yourself unconditionally.

This is the era of your outer reality mirroring the inner reality you so carefully nurtured.

This is your era of saying goodbye to the past.

This is your era of stepping into the future you've patiently waited for.

This is your time.

This is your era.

The traumas you experienced, the countless disappointments you've faced,

and the ugly projections of others don't define who you are.

They never did.

It's one thing to hear the saying,

"hurt people, hurt people", but it's another to realize,

"I don't have to be one of those people."

The cycle ends with you!

Will it be easy? Hell no.

Will it be worth it?! Absolutely.

Just because your family, malicious people, or even well-intentioned people have hurt you doesn't mean your future will be the same.

That doesn't mean your love for yourself can't blossom,

and the people that gravitate toward you won't blossom along with you.

That doesn't mean you can't start from scratch and say,

"Screw the past. I'm creating my own reality."

Nothing gets to define you but you.

So, who will you choose to be?

Come back to love.

Come back to softening your eyes and being open to seeing the magic hidden within Darkness.

Come back to your inner child that yearns for healthy communication and endless possibilities.

Come back to the world and back outside of the protective walls you've built.

You may have been preventing yourself from being hurt,

but you were also preventing yourself from experiencing genuine connections.

Come back to taking chances.

Come back to believing in magic.

Come back to taking a risk on someone that's also taking a chance on you.

Come back to what you truly deserve.

Love isn't a prison.

Love isn't a cage.

Love isn't control.

Love isn't a race.

Love is freedom.

Love is letting go and having faith.

Love is becoming one while independently embracing your own space.

Love is feeling at home within boredom.

Love is the excitement away from routines.

Love is defining from your experiences what Love can genuinely mean.

Love is YOU.

Love is ME.

Love is US when we decide that nothing ever comes between.

Look at you-

all that fiery passion with a side of no more fucks to give.

I see you.

You don't have to pretend anymore.

You're safe, you're protected, you're gifted,

and you were never meant to be accepted by everyone.

It's okay that you're too much to bear for most.

You walk on your own path,

which is lonely at times,

but I promise it's going to pay off.

So, keep going.

I have faith in you,

and deep down,

I know you do too.

you got this.

You're suspicious to people that can't even trust themselves.

Ironic, isn't it?

You're so empowered and committed to yourself that people are suspicious of you because society is too afraid to be themselves.

But we both know that's not the case, is it?

You're so real and genuine that you don't even know how to be anyone but yourself.

It's too exhausting for you to play the little mind games of society.

It's too exhausting and a waste of energy for you to pretend to like and be someone you're not.

For you, if it's not authentic and full of reciprocation,

it's not worth your time.

You're so sure of yourself that others are forced to face their insecurities,

but don't ever let that keep you from shining as bright as you can.

Pick and choose your battles.

There are times when being the bigger person and holding your composure is called for,

but then there are times when you must take a stand for who you are and your beliefs.

When it comes to blatant, harsh, and even sneaky disrespect,

at times,

it can be wiser to "choose violence."

It can be wiser to stand up and say,

"No. You are to never talk to or treat me that way.

Either alter your behavior or leave me alone."

You don't always have to be the bigger person.

You don't always have to brush off the negativity of others.

You're powerful and deserving of so much more than that,

and some people must be taught that you're no one to mess with.

Kindness isn't a weakness and isn't something to be taken for grant-ed.

Somewhere along the line,

we lose touch with what we truly deserve and become involved with a love that doesn't reflect what we truly need.

Somewhere along the line,

it takes negative experiences to remind us of just how much we've been settling, but the truth is,

you deserve someone who makes tomorrow's worries and stresses feel light and insignificant.

Someone that makes you feel like a little kid again.

Someone that loves having fun with you just as much as they love building your lives with each other.

Someone that looks at you and thinks,

"THEM!!! That's who I unquestionably want!"

Someone that says,

"I don't care what happens, we'll figure it out together."

You deserve someone that deserves you.

I finally found myself from within the deepening void of you, and I-

Being forced to learn the importance of needing myself more than someone else.

Being forced to feel the loss of a future that never came to fruition.

A future that felt so possible. So real.

Like something we've already experienced before, but it wasn't real.

It was just in my head-

and what hurts the most is that I'm not sure if you saw it too, but at least I'd like to think so.

Now, here we are.

So close to everlasting love but universes away from experiencing its whole creation-

but maybe, in another lifetime.

For now, this is goodbye, my love.

Just you watch.

This is only the beginning of your beautiful journey.

Starting now, this is where you'll begin to graciously step into who you gloriously are.

Starting now, this is where you'll continuously remind yourself that the past is dead,

the future is bright, and the present is more alive than ever.

As for the people that hurt and did you wrong?

Dead.

Those situations that almost broke you?

Dead.

Those nights you spent feeling hopeless and shattered?

DEAD.

Starting now, you're choosing to embrace that you're a warrior, and the past isn't something that holds you back but instead propels you towards your destiny.

Starting now, you are the badass you always needed.

Oh, just you watch.

You want to know what I love about you?

I love how when most of the world would have been down for the count,

you mysteriously still find a way to keep rising,

even when everyone would perfectly understand if you didn't.

You're not normal.

You realize that, right?

Your tears transmute into liquid gold.

Your sacrifices transform into infinite blessings.

Your past has been burned to ashes and then buried beneath a tombstone that reads,

"Here lies the remains of those who would have buried me here if they had their way."

If it was you vs. infinity, time would still be on your side.

You're a born winner. Embrace it.

Thank you so much for giving me a chance to experience genuine love.

Thank you for all the beautiful memories that mean so much more to me than you'll ever know.

Thank you for laughing with me and being by my side late into our restless nights.

Thank you for helping me experience a love most people dream of.

Thank you for the gentle kisses and warmth you shared while I was struggling to hold love for myself.

Thank you for showing me what love could ultimately be,

regardless of how much it would end up hurting.

If I had to choose, I'd do it all over again.

With all my entire heart, thank you.

I fell in love with my abundant growth.

I fell in love with knowing there's so much depth to my soul.

I fell in love with the endless possibilities hidden in tomorrow's day.

I fell in love with the endless amounts of love that boils within my heart.

I fell in love with my mysterious shadows.

I fell in love with my irresistible light.

I fell in love with my beautiful flaws.

I fell in love with my imperfect imperfections.

I fell in love with myself,

and damn,

does it feel amazing.

Enjoy the version of you that you currently are because one day,

you'll look back at this person very fondly.

You'll look back and be proud of how you used every last bit of your energy and courage to overcome each exhausting obstacle.

You'll give yourself a hug and kiss while looking into the mirror and tearfully pointing at yourself, saying,

"You fucking did that. YOU did!"

I assure you that nothing is ever truly hopeless when wholeheartedly embracing the life you deserve to experience.

I assure you better days are ahead of you.

I assure you that magic does, in fact, exist.

You ARE magic.

You CAN create a reality you'll be grateful for.

Each day is an opportunity for you to step forward into blessings,

and one day you'll be so grateful you began this journey in the first place.

I wish for you to know what it's like to be with someone who truly values you.

I wish for you to be chosen over and over and over again.

I wish for your heart to be safely guarded, cherished, and protected by someone who won't make the same mistakes as your past experiences.

I wish for you to feel so deeply and incredibly loved that your heart cries tears of joy and relief for its new home.

I wish for your past to be just that, the past.

I wish for your clean slate to be filled with genuine and gentle care.

I wish for your tears of sadness and disappointment to be replaced by tears of gratitude and excitement.

I wish for you to live in peace and stability.

I wish for the moment when you smile and say, "It was all worth it."

Motivation?

No, this is anything but that.

This is the next evolution of your identity.

This is the spark to awaken the super volcano that secretly lies dormant within you.

This is the eye-opening realization that the past life you grip ever so tightly between your fingers is nothing more than an illusion of sand.

This is the empowering moment you gaze into the mirror and realize your reflection was never broken or distorted.

You were just looking into the wrong mirror this entire time.

That reflection was never yours to begin with.

It was given to you by your family, friends, and society.

Now is the time you finally take back ownership of your reflection.

Now is when you stop making excuses and take accountability for your life.

You are perfectly imperfect.

There's perfection in owning your story and not being ashamed of it.

There's perfection in how you're such a beautiful mess.

There's perfection in your darkest and brightest moments.

There's perfection in your tears of sadness and bouts of joy.

There's perfection in accepting your mistakes and your willingness to learn from them.

There's perfection in the fact that there's only one YOU!

When someone shows you their true colors,

believe them.

Their actions have already spoken for their empty promises.

They've already shown you they don't have the capacity to respect your boundaries, let alone their own.

At times,

you may fall into the trap of being entranced by hallow guarantees,

but eventually,

your need for people with integrity and accountability strengthens.

Say no to tolerating half-assed people,

Say no to people that aren't committed to backing up their words,

and start saying yes to respecting yourself and the priceless value you hold.

No more excuses,

No more trying to fit in.

No more making yourself smaller.

No more running away from your problems.

No more letting disrespect slide.

No more investing in people that don't back up their words with actions.

And no more waiting for people to change when you've been ready to move forward.

You've been selling yourself short,

and that's NOT okay.

You've been sacrificing steps from your own journey for people that wouldn't bat an eye if you hit rock bottom.

Some people hope you don't realize just how special and impactful you are,

but I think it's time you start owning it and putting on a show.

It's time you SHINE.

Little did I know,

I needed to lose you to find myself.

No matter how much frustration I felt from how things turned out-

at the end of the day,

it's still all love and always will be.

So, thank you.

Thank you for showing me what it truly means to love myself.

Thank you for showing me what I genuinely deserve.

Thank you for showing me that you can never have everlasting love
if fear is in the way.

Thank you for not being what I wanted, but for being what I needed
at the time.

Thank you for pushing me to become a more evolved version of
myself.

What people don't tell you about growth is how lonely and over-whelming it can be.

In the process, you lose friends, comfort, stability, things you used to love, and even yourself.

Self-growth appears so shiny, exciting, and pretty on the outside,

but sometimes can feel anything but that.

Self-growth isn't a journey for the weak, and even if you aren't, it still manages to break you into tiny pieces that are unrecognizable compared to who you were before.

Stepping into a manifested reality isn't something that can be half-assed.

It calls for every fiber of your being.

It calls for you to become something more significant than yourself.

More remarkable than everything you've ever known-

but even with everything being said, it's a path I would choose over and over.

So, are you with me?

You're an incredibly passionate lover and a relentlessly resilient fighter.

It's not in you to back down from whatever it is that purely speaks to your heart.

It's not in you to not pour your entire essence out into the ethers of the Universe.

It's not in you to just simply "get by."

You're here for a reason,

and it isn't just to experience what it means to survive.

You're here to soar throughout the galaxies.

Your blood, sweat, and tears will create the most beautiful experiences and moments for yourself and others.

Your entire existence will be devoted to embracing love in a world that so desperately tries to hate.

You are everything this world needs,

and it's time you start accepting that.

You thought you were hurting me,

but you were only hurting yourself.

The truth is, I'm okay.

I always have been and always will be.

I know my worth,

so, when someone betrays me,

I know it isn't personal and is just a reflection of how they feel about themselves.

I know that your self-sabotaging was because you were afraid of peace.

You were afraid of stillness.

You were afraid of being happy.

So, instead of trusting this would work,

you already had one foot out the door before it even began.

It's okay, though.

I forgive you.

I hope you heal sooner than later,

and I hope you learn to forgive yourself as well.

Farewell.

Your heart and soul are way too valuable to be met by people who are set on misunderstanding you before they even hear you.

They are way too valuable to be met through the mind games of those that are too insecure about expressing themselves healthily and freely.

They deserve to connect with souls who not only value themselves but aren't hesitant to make sure you feel valued as well.

At the center of who you are lies the essence of pure love and life itself.

You are the physical embodiment of the love the Universe creatively expresses.

Who you are is proof that magic exists.

The point of forgiving someone that hurt you isn't to release them from what they've done.

It's to release YOU from what they've done.

Forgiving someone is saying,

"Thank you for helping me realize my worth by showing me what I don't deserve."

It's saying,

"Thank you for showing me where I need to heal so I can only accept connections that are healthy and that truly bring me value."

It's saying,

"Thank you for helping me reevaluate what deserves to have a space in my life and what doesn't."

Forgiving someone gives you a chance to let it go so you can create the space for better things to come into your life.

Release yourself from their actions.

That pain is not yours to carry and has no business being brought into your future.

I haven't been honest.

I'm afraid.

I'm afraid of loving so deeply that I'll never be able to reach the surface if I am ever betrayed again.

I'm afraid of being truly close to anyone because closeness for me has almost entirely led to hurtful experiences and heartaches.

I'm afraid of being completely honest and vulnerable with people that only care to take advantage of the endless love I have to offer,

but more than being afraid, I've realized that I'm brave.

My vulnerabilities, openness, and kindness are something the world and I need.

They're superpowers, and with these powers, those little fears can be gently nurtured and told,

"It's okay. You can finally rest. You've done your job."

And that tiny possibility of things going in my favor is worth the risk-

EVERY. SINGLE. TIME.

I'm afraid,

but I'll be brave while I do it anyways.

The things you used to believe don't have to be what you embody anymore.

Set yourself free of those shackles.

Break free of those repressive patterns.

You are so much more than your experiences and traumas.

You are so much more than who people perceive you to be.

At the end of the day,

the only opinion of yourself that truly matters is your own.

What will you choose for that opinion to be?

Something that only hurts you and binds you?

Or something beautiful and liberating?

It's your choice, love.

Choose wisely.

It's quiet.

The thought of you no longer makes a sound.

Destruction in my mind where you'd manipulate and plot,

trying to take advantage of someone who foolishly cared so much
for you,

but that someone no longer exists.

It makes you feel sad, doesn't it?

Well good.

I hope you feel as foolish as I once did,

and hopefully, you'll learn from your mistakes,

but it's no longer my place to care what happens from here on out.

How you deal with your guilt isn't my responsibility anymore.

Now, I'm free.

Sometimes,

walking away from the past just isn't enough.

Sometimes,

you must leave,

explore the deepest parts of you that you once felt ashamed to embrace,

come back stronger than before,

and then burn it entirely to the ground.

That doesn't mean there weren't plenty of moments to be cherished,

it means that sometimes,

you must completely dismantle 'what was'-

to create something more wonderful than you could have ever imagined.

It means that your past doesn't define you,

never did,

and never will.

Maybe,

the point of healing isn't to find a "fix" but to learn how to carry your pain in a way that brings you more joyful experiences than hurtful ones.

Maybe,

the point is to forgive yourself for the actions of others without needing to also forgive them.

Maybe,

the point is to realize that the life you used to know doesn't have to be the life you continue to know moving forward-

and though your heart was shattered into a million little pieces,

that doesn't mean you are broken.

Instead,

you were always whole,

regardless of how that appears.

Maybe,

the point of healing is to reclaim your power from the narrative of what it means to be you.

Always remember, you are the prize.

But just as importantly,

you deserve to have a partner you'd be proud to call your equal.

Someone who shares your value for compassion and respect.

Someone who honors their words and your heart,

regardless of whether you are skin-to-skin or planets apart.

Someone who wakes up next to you during a peaceful summer night and asks,

"Wow. I get to experience this?

I get to experience you?"

You deserve a partner you can passionately build a future with one moment,

then laugh like little kids the next.

You deserve a love that undyingly deserves you.

You're one of the world's greatest secrets.

From your sweet smile that rarely visits to say hi,

to your innocent laughter that could soften any heart of stone.

You are a hidden gem among an ecosystem of infertile dirt.

Who you are is a blessing to this cursed existence,

and the world may not deserve you,

but **YOU** do.

You deserve to shine every single day,

and I'm so sorry you were ever pushed to feel otherwise,

but being true to who you are is the most beautiful thing you can ever do.

Thank you so much for existing.

I tried to help save you from your darker days,

but little did I know you never actually intended on changing for the better.

Secretly,

you intended to devote yourself towards a path of self-destruction-

a path with no remorse for those caught within the debris of the life you were burning down.

But over time,

I came to realize that loving you was a form of self-destruction.

I didn't value myself enough to know when I loved in vain,

because at the time,

the breadcrumbs were just enough to keep me returning for more.

It got to the point where I could no longer point the finger at you and had to take accountability for allowing myself to settle.

And with that accountability came a new journey toward saving myself and growing toward everything truly meant for me.

I couldn't save you.

So, I saved myself instead.

Look into the mirror and say these things to yourself even if you don't believe them at this moment:

"You aren't responsible for how people misplace your heart and trust."

"You aren't responsible for the healing of others. You are only responsible for your own."

"It's not your responsibility to understand why people decided to hurt you. It's your job to value yourself regardless and to choose YOU."

"Your heart and mind are so beautiful, and I'm so lucky to be you. I love you so much."

"I'm so proud of you for how far you've come, despite all the pain you've experienced."

"Thank you for existing. Thank you for always taking care of me."

You hear that, don't you?

That fire that blazes within your chest.

That warrior that screams out after surviving moments you were sure you'd die from.

Do you realize who the fuck you are?

This isn't a game.

You're no one to be played with.

You're an absolute monster in the most beautiful ways possible.

Your existence is proof that terrible nothings can evolve into extravagant something's.

You're the living, breathing definition of a miracle.

Be grateful that you are who you are.

Your story is just beginning.

You're not like them.

Wake up.

I know it's been lonely,

I know it's been chaotic,

and I know it's been confusing,

but let me bring you some clarity.

This was meant to happen.

YOU were meant to happen.

In order to rediscover yourself,

you had to be isolated from everyone else.

You had to learn to pour your love into yourself to shine brightly
and pour your love into those who need you.

You matter.

Your voice matters.

Your life essence matters.

People need you.

The world needs you.

The Universe needs you.

Wake up.

If your teardrops could speak,

they'd tell you how much of an incredible job you've been doing.

They'd tell you how beautifully graceful you've been while flowing through these challenging times.

They'd tell you how much they unconditionally love you and that they couldn't be any prouder that you somehow stand with your head held high, despite all odds.

They'd tell you that it's okay to rest and to take all the time you need and that the world will patiently wait for your essential return.

They'd tell you that they wouldn't want to roll down the precious cheeks of anyone else.

That they feel right at home,

no matter how horrible you feel.

If your teardrops could speak,

they'd say that you're never alone and that they'll ALWAYS be there to embrace you when you need them.

Welcome to your villain era.

Welcome to your era of transmuting your painful nights into fuel that lights your path toward what feeds your soul.

Welcome to your era of shutting the door on people and experiences that refused to value your indomitable spirit.

Welcome to your empowering new beginning born from the ashes of much-needed endings.

This isn't your time to passively go with the flow.

This is your time to BECOME the flow.

This is your time to powerfully shift your energetic currents toward decisive decisions.

This is your time to reevaluate,

get rid of,

and make room for what holds space within your life.

Remember,

everyone's a villain in someone's story,

so, embrace it.

Be the villain.

I respect my worth because I have to.

Throughout life I gave my love and energy so freely because I believed that others would be more than happy to do the same,

but sadly, I discovered that wasn't the case.

I discovered that when something is given so freely, regardless of its actual value, the chances of it being treated with carelessness grow exponentially.

The reality of it is sad, isn't it?!

But it's the truth.

People won't treat you with care and respect if you don't treat yourself with care and respect.

Love yourself,

hold firm boundaries,

hold yourself to a high standard,

and always remember-

Being a loving soul doesn't mean you have to love any less.

It just means you must be more aware of how and to whom you give that love.

We're manifesting a love so effortless that the pages of our intimate story magically turn themselves.

A love that periodically checks in by asking,

"Is there anything I could be doing to help you feel more valued, seen, or appreciated?"

We're manifesting the love we always wished for, not the kind from movies,

but the love we KNOW is real and is completely specific to us.

Someone who consistently cares for healthy communication, understanding, and deeper alignment.

We're manifesting someone who doesn't care if the "grass is greener" because they're unequivocally devoted to nurturing their world with us.

We're manifesting what our heart and soul always needed.

We're manifesting a love that's so beautifully human, yet divine.

You're not who everyone thinks you are or expects you to be.

You're so much deeper than that.

Those old habits, experiences, and mindsets-

They're not you anymore. They're long gone.

Sure, they'll always be a part of your story, but you're doing yourself an injustice by trying to fit into the life of someone who doesn't presently exist.

Live up to who you are IN THIS MOMENT.

YOU'RE FREE!

Give your hugs, say your goodbyes, cry your tears, mourn your fears, and get ready for a new adventure that's created by YOU.

I need for you to trust yourself.

I believe in you.

You got this.

I gave you parts of me I never knew existed.

I shared with you my darkest secrets and my most beautiful memories.

I gave you moments of clarity and stillness within your episodes of chaos.

I gave you my entire world and it still wasn't enough,

but I realized that it wasn't on me.

I realized that nothing would ever be enough for someone that just isn't meant for you.

I realized that healthy reciprocation is so much more important than loving someone just for the sake of loving someone.

I realized that patience in finding a partner that can mirror the healthy kind of love you need is a must.

And lastly,

I realized that the things I need and desire for me are non-negotiable,

and it's perfectly okay to have high standards.

Who are you at heart?

You're someone extremely caring, full of imagination, and have a cup of love so deep that the bottom has yet to be reached by any of humankind.

You're compassionate.

You're a Dragon.

You're someone who will never give up,

even after your last breath has left your body.

You don't back down.

You accept life's challenges and take accountability for how you handle life experiences.

Your trust in yourself is building into a skyscraper that reaches beyond the stars.

The belief and hope you have in people is ingrained into your DNA.

You believe in magic.

You ARE magic.

Who you are at heart is someone the world and you truly need and deserve.

Do this. Do that. Heal this. Change that.

Blah blah blah.

During this journey of growth and stepping into the life you deserve,

it's hard to not get swept up in the need to constantly be doing something.

Amidst all the chaos of sorting through your thoughts, emotions, relationships, passions, traumas, and countless other things-

it's important to remember that one of the most productive things you could ever do is NOTHING.

Give yourself a break. Give your mind a break.

Take some days, or even weeks, to just put down those worries and spend time in nature and disconnect from the world.

Spend time reconnecting to your soul.

Spend time reconnecting to your own power.

You work hard enough.

Please, enjoy some much-needed time for yourself.

It wasn't your fault.

The blame and resentment projected towards you weren't yours to carry.

I'm so sorry you've been carrying this crushing weight,

but I'm here to tell you that it's okay now.

You can finally put it down.

You were the target of someone else's guilt and shame.

You were shattered by someone else's brokenness.

It wasn't your fault.

It wasn't your responsibility.

And now it's safe to let it go and cry it out.

You are so loved.

The people you should be surrounding yourself with are the ones who speak to your heart and soul.

It should be the people that don't see vulnerability and openness as weaknesses but as a sign of trust and strength.

It should be the people that choose to embrace love and connections-

even though their experiences have tried to convince them to close off their hearts.

It's the people who happily respect your time, space, and boundaries.

The people you should be surrounding yourself with from now on are the ones who reflect the best parts of you, while healthily encouraging you to heal and grow.

I always wondered who I'd be if I never chose me.

I always wondered who I'd be if I let society package me into a tidy little box. So neat. So perfect. So afraid to embrace how much of a beautiful mess I can be.

I always wondered what would've happened if I had never stopped people-pleasing and didn't listen to my heart.

I always wondered who I'd be if I never questioned the ordinary and did what everyone else said was the "right" thing to do.

I always wondered what would've happened if I had settled for "good enough" and didn't believe that true love existed.

I always wondered,

but I guess we'll never know.

Her reign leaves a trail of fire and Darkness every once in a Blue Moon.

Since a young age, she witnessed the cyclical and unfair treatment that shrouded the people around her.

"I refuse. That will not be my reality. My destiny is to break free of these horrendous chains."

And so, she did, day by daunting day.

She chose to be an anomaly.

She chose to be a self-empowered leader.

She's a firm believer that people were brainwashed into drowning out their inner inferno for the sake of the fragile egos of those in power.

She's the living, breathing reminder that the silenced eventually become the silencers.

She's a breaker of chains.

She's a Goddess of Dragons.

Every time you say yes to something else but no to yourself, the 'you' on the inside takes note of that.

They take note of the fact that they're not being heard.

They take note of the fact that they aren't receiving better treatment.

They take note of the fact you're not listening to them and that their voice doesn't seem as important.

The relationship you have with yourself is real.

The relationship with yourself is what affects your confidence, your self-esteem, and your trust in yourself.

If it doesn't feel right, say no or quietly remove yourself from the situation.

If you feel you're being taken advantage of, walk away immediately.

If you're not feeling valued or seen, be sure to SEE YOURSELF.

There's nothing more important than the relationship you have with yourself.

Please, don't take it for granted.

To the right person, you don't have to change yourself to be attractive and lovable.

You don't have to beg or convince that you're worth the frictions of growth.

You don't even have to be "good enough."

Your depths and existence ARE already good enough.

The person you are, the love that flows within you, and the heaviness of the burdens you've carried are enough.

The right person will mean it when they say,

"To me, there's nothing in this world that is more valuable than you."

Reality is what you make it,

and you have so much more power than you realize.

There is power in having faith that magic IS real.

There is power in realizing that you ARE magic.

Your life energy is magic.

The fact that you're alive is magic.

There is power in believing you'll be okay no matter what happens.

That no matter what, you can do absolutely ANYTHING.

There is power in letting go of control and surrendering to the beautiful energy life will continuously bring your way.

There is power in being open to new opportunities and circumstances.

There is power in acknowledging that your past experiences were valid,

but they served their purpose and *have no room in the new life you're creating.*

It's funny, isn't it?

People look at you and see a precious little diamond who is so gentle and kind,

but they're only seeing a small part of the picture.

They don't see the remains of the shadows that tried to suffocate you as you ran toward your problems.

They don't see the assertiveness you've adopted to put manipulators in their place.

They don't see the Dragon that miraculously rose from the ashes,

even though Darkness was sure you were buried for good.

Who you are is an enigma.

Who you are is beauty in its purest form.

Who you are is mystical.

People look at you in awe,

and you simply smile in return.

"One day at a time, huh?"

Yeah, one day at a time.

"Aren't you afraid?"

I'm absolutely terrified...

but I wouldn't have it any other way.

'Being afraid' means I'm doing something truly worth fighting for.

'Being afraid' means I'm fully embracing what it means for me to be alive,

and if 'being afraid' is the only thing that's between me and what I desire,

then I'm running towards fear-

Every. Single. Time.

You must learn to accept the inevitability that your growth will trigger others.

Some people will become envious.

They'll jealously question how someone they perceive as inferior to them is somehow evolving in ways they have trouble imagining.

Some people will feel left out.

They'll believe that your choice to choose yourself means that they're not good enough.

And some will do their best to tear you down.

They'll talk about how you think you're better than everyone,

they'll twist your words,

and they'll lie in hopes people will turn their backs on you.

But the thing is,

how others feel about your growth is NOT your responsibility.

Your responsibility is to follow your heart and give your all to the life you envision while attracting people that also desire the same.

Your responsibility is to embrace who you are unapologetically and never look back.

When someone is disloyal to you, it doesn't mean you aren't good enough.

It means that they believe that THEY aren't good enough.

It means they don't value or trust themselves enough to be loyal to anyone, not even themselves.

It means that they don't respect themselves, so they can't have respect for you.

It means that their impulsiveness shows they have a lack of self-control.

Why would you even want to be with someone that doesn't have enough self-control to simply be loyal and honest?

You were never asking for too much. You were just asking the wrong person.

It says everything about them and nothing about you.

You're amazing just the way you are.

You've always been good enough.

You're truly unique and irreplaceable.

No one can utterly say or do the things you do-

many imitate,

but they're always missing that one special ingredient...

YOU.

From your mannerisms, to the way your eyes dance around the room as you search for words that could never do your mind justice,

to the ways your voice and energy levitates whenever you're struck by a bolt of passion,

and to your soul of sunlight that infinitely pours into the things you love-

*there's simply, no one quite like **you**.*

Little by little,

piece by piece,

I learned I was never broken but always complete.

The thoughts of overthinking who I was and what I deserved
were slowly replaced by unconditional love for myself and priceless
self-worth.

It was so dark at times that I thought I'd always be blind,

but little did I know the beautiful light I would find.

My sadness turned into bliss,

and my tears turned into a strength.

It was sink or swim in the vast depths of doubt,

and I fought not to sink.

I know who I am now,

and I'm amazed at who I was always meant to be.

Little by little,

piece by piece,

I learned that the "peace" I needed was always inside of me.

-dedicated to my dear friend and magical little fairy, Christina O.

You have so much power within you that you have yet to realize.

That anger that burns intensely in your chest?

Use that as your fuel to create positive change.

That sadness that weighs heavily within your heart?

Use that as your reminder that more beautiful things are yet to come.

That loneliness you try to hide behind your eyes?

Use that as your strength of independence which holds your head high regardless of what anyone else says.

And that pain that aches within your soul?

Use that as your brush to repaint a mural of healing for yourself and the world.

Your "weaknesses" are your strengths.

Don't let them go to waste.

I believe in you.

They weren't feeling guilty when they assumed you were at your worst.

They weren't feeling guilty when they thought other options were better than you.

They weren't feeling guilty when creating false stories about who you are.

But now they feel guilty because they realize you're better off without their manipulative ways.

They feel guilty because they're afraid you've realized how much power and light you hold.

They feel guilty because they've realized they hurt someone who genuinely valued and cared for them-

but that guilt isn't for you to carry.

It's theirs.

Breathe in,

grow from your lessons,

breathe out,

and let it all go.

You're finally free.

It's a nonnegotiable that you're seen and accepted as the priceless work of art you are.

You're no trophy.

You're no accomplishment.

You're so much more than that.

You're too real, too bare, and too convoluted to ever be reduced into a bite-size caricature of yourself.

You were messily but beautifully reborn from within the cosmic explosion of your vivacious heart.

You were brought back together from within the voids of your once-shattered hopes and dreams.

You weren't warmly embraced by the sun and care of loving souls but were instead molded by your own two determined hands,

even though you were blinded by a shroud of darkness.

You're someone that needs to be met where you are.

You've shared endless love with yourself,

and you'd be foolish to accept anything less than that.

You're beautiful.

You're powerful.

You're elegance in physical form.

Who you are is priceless.

This isn't like you,

the real you.

You may not entirely be there yet, but who you are is way more than enough for this world.

Who you are is someone that needs to be seen.

Just because there have been certain people from your past who weren't accepting of you or expected you to be smaller than who you are,

that doesn't mean there are not plenty of people out there that would be filled with joy to see the real you.

That doesn't mean that who you always were at your core wasn't someone that was deeply needed by this world.

The real you never needed permission or validation from anyone but you.

Who you are is so very special, and from deep within my heart, I hope these words sink into yours.

Who you are is someone that absolutely needs to be set free,

so please, set yourself free.

I had to let you go so we could grab ahold of ourselves in places we were falling apart.

I hated that I caused you heartbreak by breaking away,

but this was the best choice for us both.

You'll probably hate me for the rest of our lives,

and I get why.

You saw me as your best friend,

someone you could experience and share the beautiful,

the ugly,

and the mundane.

I was that person for you,

but I had to break away because I realized we weren't growing healthily together.

We were just together for the sake of being together,

and it was hurting us.

It wasn't you.

It wasn't me.

It was just life.

Love is never easy. Love is never perfect.

Love is when your differences don't separate what's worth it.

Love is unconditionally accepting someone as they are while encouraging them to fly until they shine among the stars.

Love is celebrating even in your darkest moments,

and when problems bring you closer,

not turn you into opponents.

Love is falling deeper after landing on your feet.

Love is having faith through all the uncertainties you see.

Love is something that simply makes sense when it is right.

Don't deny yourself the most beautifully incredible ride of your life.

The person you are and the love you carry is a bottomless pool of vibrancy.

Your vibrancy scares most people into feeling like they're not good enough,

and then not feeling good enough urges them to self-sabotage something healthy for them.

But you're worthy of loyalty and commitment regardless of them being afraid.

Never settle until someone is more than happy to take up the responsibility of reciprocating what you deserve.

True love isn't a feeling.

Instead,

it's what you do regardless of your feelings.

You deserve nice things.

You deserve beautiful experiences.

Not because you've "earned" them.

Not because you proved that you are "worthy,"

but because your existence is simply already enough.

You don't have to prove anything to anyone to be deserving.

Society tricks us by having so many metrics to say if we're worthy,

and it's absolute bullshit.

Your bank account, your popularity, your social status, your looks, your job-

they mean absolutely nothing.

Who you are is already enough,

*and that's **ALWAYS** been the case.*

I hope one day you're able to say no to what feels wrong and exclaim "YES!!" to what feels excitedly natural to you.

I hope you walk away from everything that drains you and instead run towards whatever encourages you to take up space and shine as brightly as you so desperately deserve.

I hope you're seen for exactly who you wish to grow into and become as magical as the version of yourself you dream of within your waking moments.

One day you will look at your reflection and smile at how incredibly proud you are of yourself.

I hope one day you realize that you've always been needed and desired by the right people,

and anything that made you feel less deserving truly doesn't matter.

It's healthy to feel your sadness.

It's healthy to acknowledge you feel lonely.

It's healthy to feel anger towards things that aren't right for you.

These darker feelings help us to see things that may need to be changed.

They help us to evolve.

They help us to feel grounded.

Darkness can provide you strength,

transformation,

and even life-changing results,

but it's not something to be made a permanent home out of.

You need to have a fluid balance between Darkness and Light,

otherwise,

your perception will tilt too far to either side-

and you'll become blind to the other half of life.

I remember those lonely nights of despair so clearly to this day.

From life experiences, my heart was shattered into a million pieces, and each shallow breath I took as I cried only appeared to multiply those pieces.

While I sat on the grass at 3 a.m., I rocked back and forth as I hugged myself around my knees, desperately trying to give myself the embrace I yearned for from a world that seemingly failed me.

"When will it end? I'm so tired, and my heart hurts so much it physically aches."

I didn't know where to go, but my eyes stayed glued to the train tracks in front of me as a possible escape.

"No. I can't do that. There are people here that will have to deal with the aftermath of my choice, and I can't do that to them."

"I don't want to leave yet," I cried, looking up to the dark, faceless sky.

I had absolutely no proof that things would improve, but I had to try with my entire soul.

I at least owed my broken heart that much.

That night I learned that unshakable hope CAN be cultivated within Darkness.

I let my emotions fuel my will to live. I let my sorrows create abundance. I let my weaknesses become my strengths.

We didn't come this far to only come this far. We came this far to go further than we ever imagined was possible. We came this far because life is what we make it, and *we're choosing to make it beautiful*.

The Moon will always have our hearts.

There's something comforting about how Darkness and shadows naturally feel like a safe space for our most bizarre dreams and dearest secrets.

There's something mystical about how the Moon softly illuminates our scars and fears so clearly for us to notice and challenge.

There's something so breathtaking about diving within the deepest parts of our souls while learning how to trust ourselves in ways that make us feel like we're finally breathing for the first time.

For those of us miraculously raised from within the darkest of voids,

we carry gifts that help us to see through the deceptions of manipulators and pretenders.

We have been given powers to illuminate truths within this world.

We are entrusted with empowering those lost on their way through The Abyss.

We've been given the power to guide others toward becoming aware of the ugly realities of life while teaching them to remain open to the wondrously beautiful possibilities of our present moments and futures.

For many of us, this is a fresh new beginning.

This is where we finally look Darkness in the eyes and say,

"Here I am. I'm no longer afraid.

I no longer deny who I was always meant to be.

I belong here, and I'm here to stay."

This is where we finally take ownership of our lives and circumstances and choose to take a stand.

This is where we evolve.

As Warriors and Dragons of the Moon,

we will change ourselves and this world for the better,

one beautifully dark and twisted night at a time.

JUSTIN TRINITY is a writer from Chicago.

Thank you for sharing your time, energy, and courage.

instagram.com/justin.trinity

tiktok.com/justin.trinity

justintrinityxo@gmail.com

Ingram Content Group UK Ltd.
Milton Keynes UK
UKHW021005260723
425798UK00011B/64